LEWIS HAMILTON

UNAUTHORISED BIOGRAPHY

John Townsend

www.raintreepublishers.co.uk
Visit our website to find out more information about Raintree books.

To order:
☎ Phone 44 (0) 1865 888112
▤ Send a fax to 44 (0) 1865 314091
▥ Visit the Raintree bookshop at www.raintreepublishers.co.uk to browse our catalogue and order online.

Raintree is an imprint of Pearson Education Limited, a company incorporated in England and Wales having its registered office at Edinburgh Gate, Harlow, Essex, CM20 2JE – Registered company number: 00872828

Raintree is a registered trademark of Pearson Education Limited

Editorial: Catherine Veitch
Design: Richard Parker and Q2A Solutions
Illustrations: Oxford Designers and Illustrators
Picture research: Mica Brancic
Production: Victoria Fitzgerald

Originated by Dot Gradations Ltd
Printed in China by CTPS

ISBN 978 1 4062 0953 2
12 11 10 09 08
10 9 8 7 6 5 4 3 2 1

British Library Cataloguing in Publication Data
Townsend, John
Lewis Hamilton. – (Sport files)
796.7'2'092
A full catalogue record for this book is available from the British Library.

Acknowledgements
We would like to thank the following for permission to reproduce photographs: © Action Images pp. **9** (DPPI/Jacky Foulatier), **13** (Crispin Thruston); Getty Images pp. **11** (Sion Touhig), **15** (AFP/William West), **22** (AFP Photo/Chris Young), **26** (AFP Photo/Lionel Cironneau), **27** (AFP Photo/William West); © Reuters/Jason Reed/Action Images p. **5**; © Rex Features pp. **7** (Philip Brown), **8** (Anglia Press Agency Ltd.), **10** (Damien McFadden), **16** (Sipa Press), **19** (Ken McKay), **20** (Nils Jorgensen), **21** (Julian Makey), **23** (Jonathan Hordle), **24** (Giuliano Bevilacqua), **25** (Chris Ratcliffe).

Cover photograph of Lewis Hamilton reproduced with permission of ©Getty Images (Mark Thompson).

Every effort has been made to contact copyright holders of material reproduced in this book. Any omissions will be rectified in subsequent printings if notice is given to the publishers.

CONTENTS

Some words are shown in bold, **like this.** You can find out what they mean by looking in the glossary.

Imagine what it must be like to drive a **Formula One** racing car at almost 320 kph (200 mph). Every Formula One car on the **starting grid** can shoot from 0–160 kph (100 mph) in less than 5 seconds. The power from the engine is amazing.

Imagine the tension before the start of the race, the smell of fumes, the scream of the engine, the burst of speed. Then the roar of the track, the yells from the crowd as you pass the chequered finishing flag ... and the spray of champagne when you win the race! A young boy used to dream of driving to victory, and climbing the **podium** as a motor racing champion. His dream came true not many years after he left school. His name is now known by millions: Lewis Hamilton.

Motor racing can be full of excitement, speed, danger, money, and glamour. Anyone who reaches the top in such a fiercely competitive sport is soon in the **media** spotlight. Racing drivers are some of the biggest superstars of the sporting world. Lewis Hamilton is one of the few drivers who won a major race in his very first season. But it's tough at the top, as he quickly found out.

At the end of the 2007 season, at just 22 years old, Lewis was only one point from becoming the World Champion. That was in his very first year in Formula One racing.

FAST FACT FILE

Name:	Lewis Carl Hamilton
Born:	7 January 1985, Stevenage, Hertfordshire
Height:	1.74 m (5 ft 8 in)
Weight:	67 kg (10st 7 lbs)
Team:	McLaren-Mercedes
First F1 grand prix:	Melbourne, Australia, March 2007
First F1 grand prix win:	Montreal, Canada, June 2007
Records:	Only driver in Formula One history to finish his first nine races on the podium. Only driver in Formula One history to score points in 15 races out of the 17 races held in his first season.

Sir Stirling Moss, the famous British racing driver who raced from 1948 to 1962, said that Lewis Hamilton is "the best thing to happen to Formula One in my time". What a tribute!

*Lewis Hamilton, the superstar of the 2007 Canadian **Grand Prix**.*

Lewis' grandparents arrived in Britain from the West Indies in 1955. At first they lived in London, then they moved to Stevenage, in Hertfordshire. Lewis' dad, Anthony, was born in Stevenage. When Anthony grew up, he married Carmen. Their first son was born in 1985, and they called him Lewis, after the US athlete Carl Lewis. In fact, they gave their son the full name of Lewis Carl Hamilton.

When Lewis was two years old his parents separated. Lewis lived with his mother at first. By the time he was five years old it was clear to everyone that Lewis loved cars. He not only loved to race radio-controlled cars, but he also wanted to drive go-karts. Lewis later went to live with his father, who encouraged him to try go-kart racing. Before long Lewis caught the racing bug.

KARTING

Go-karts are simple, small four-wheeled motor vehicles that are raced around circuits. A Formula A kart, with a 100cc engine, can accelerate from 0–96.6 kph (0–60 mph), and has a top speed of 140 kph (85 mph). Go-kart racing classes start at age seven or eight.

Lewis Hamilton's karting career highlights:
Super 1 National Cadet Champion 1995 (aged 10)
Super 1 National Formula Yamaha Champion 1997 (aged 12)
European Formula A Champion 2000 (aged 15)
World Cup Formula A Champion 2000 (aged 15)

Lewis also decided to take on another challenge. He took up karate, and by the time he was 12 he had gained a **black belt**.

At the age of 10, Lewis was the youngest karting champion in the UK.

As he grew older, Lewis' house became full of trophies. He took his racing very seriously and it wasn't long before he was winning lots of prizes. The important people in motor sport knew all about Lewis and they were keeping a close eye on him. At the age of 10, Lewis walked up to an astonished Ron Dennis, the McLaren **Formula One** team boss, and said "One day ... I'm going to race for McLaren."

Just a few years later, when Lewis was 13 years old, Mclaren signed him up to their driver development programme. The contract stated that he could eventually be considered as a Formula One driver for Mclaren. This was Lewis' dream. He was the youngest ever driver to get this type of contract.

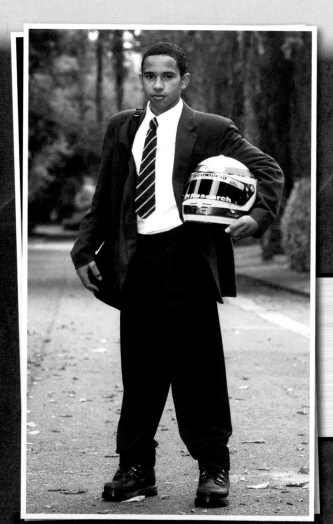

At the age of 13, Lewis trained with Mclaren after school. His dad always made Lewis wear a bright yellow helmet, so he'd be easy to find in a crash.

A hectic life

By the time he was 15 years old, Lewis had a hectic life trying to fit in school with all his training and kart racing. He had to travel around Europe to many events, so he missed a lot of school. He was keen to learn, however, so he was given home tuition, often very early in the morning. Lewis also had to fit in visits to the gym because fitness is very important for a driver. "It's hectic but it's what I want to do," said Lewis.

In 2000 Lewis took two top karting awards when he became both the European Formula A champion and the World Cup Formula A champion. The motor racing world was now taking him very seriously. It wouldn't be long now before he'd be entering the next level of motor racing, and driving the fastest racing cars.

Lewis progressed through go-karting championships until he moved on to cars in 2001.

In 2001, at the age of just 16, Lewis left go-karting behind and began his car racing career. He couldn't wait to get behind the wheel of a full-size racing car and reach even greater speeds. His team manager said, "The first time we slotted him in the car, he crashed it. Not in a ridiculous manner, it was more because he was pushing hard and enjoying the car. We got it repaired and he went straight back out."

Despite all the excitement of this new challenge, Lewis still had to keep up with his schoolwork. After all, this was his GCSE year. His school friends got used to seeing Lewis being dropped off in a **sponsored** car with his name along the side!

Lewis came third overall in the Formula Renault UK Championship Series in 2001. The famous **Formula One** racing driver, and seven-times world champion, Michael Schumacher was so amazed by the young Lewis that he said, "He's a quality driver, very strong and only 16. If he keeps this up I'm sure he will reach Formula One. It's something special to see a kid of his age out on the circuit. He's clearly got the right racing mentality."

Lewis had won many trophies even before he moved on to car racing.

Just for the record ... Lewis passed his road driving test. His first car was a Mini Cooper.

The climb to stardom

After GCSEs, Lewis studied for his A-levels at the Cambridge College of Arts and Science. Between race training and circuit meetings, fitness training, and studying Lewis had several part-time jobs. After all, he had to save up for driving lessons and his road driving test!

In 2002 Lewis had more success on the junior circuit. That year, he finished third in the British Formula Renault series and came first just a year later. But even greater things were just around the corner.

From 2003 to 2006 Lewis' driving skills improved, he entered more races, and won more trophies. But he still had to earn money. When he was 18 years old, a local Mercedes garage **sponsored** him and he sometimes worked there as a part-time **valet**. He had a real passion for cleaning cars and he kept them spotless.

Lewis got a real shock one day, when the sales manager called him over and told him there had been complaints about a car he had cleaned. Lewis was stunned, until he saw the manager smile. He led Lewis over to a shiny Mercedes sports coupe and told him: "This is yours!" Lewis couldn't believe it.

In 2004, aged 19, Lewis was racing in Formula Three (F3) events. He won one of the races in the F3 **Euroseries** and came fifth overall that year. But the following year was his big break. Lewis won the Euroseries drivers' title, as well as the Monaco F3 **Grand Prix**.

WHAT IS FORMULA THREE?

Formula Three motor racing, including the F3 Euroseries championship, is part of the "career road" for junior drivers to progress to the Formula One world championship, which is the highest form of single-seater racing. The championship consists of ten events, each comprising two races, held at a variety of European circuits. A driver's final position is determined by the number of points gained over all the events.

Lewis wins the GP2 championship on his first attempt in 2006.

Lewis hits the big time

In 2006 Lewis progressed to race in the Grand Prix 2 Series (GP2). GP2 is known as the "feeder sport" and training ground for **Formula One** racing car drivers. After an exciting GP2 championship battle lasting 20 races, Lewis won the title in the 19th race in Monza, Italy. It was a great achievement. Would Lewis' dream of driving in Formula One now become a reality?

At the end of 2006 Lewis' dream came true – he was chosen to drive for McLaren-Mercedes in **Formula One** racing. The McLaren-Mercedes manager Ron Dennis said that giving Lewis this chance was a gamble, but that he deserved this opportunity and had "earned his chance".

The races

Formula One (F1) is the highest class of motor racing. The "formula" in the name is a set of rules that all drivers and cars must meet. The F1 World Championship is a series of races, known as **Grand Prix**. The results of each race are combined to produce a winner. The British Grand Prix is part of the Formula One World Championships. It is held at Silverstone in Northamptonshire.

TOP THREE CHAMPIONS OF FORMULA ONE

Pos	Country	Driver	Race wins	F1 career	First win	Last win
1	Germany	Michael Schumacher	91 wins	1991–2006	1992 Belgian Grand Prix	2006 Chinese Grand Prix
2	France	Alain Prost	51 wins	1980–1991, 1993	1981 French Grand Prix	1993 German Grand Prix
3	Brazil	Ayrton Senna	41 wins	1984–1994	1985 Portuguese Grand Prix	1993 Australian Grand Prix

The cars

A Formula One car is a single-seat, open-**cockpit**, open-wheel racing car. Its engine sits behind the driver. Formula One rules say that cars must be constructed by the racing teams themselves. Teams such as Honda, Toyota, McLaren-Mercedes, and Ferrari can each spend about £100 million on engines in a year.

As well as being very fast when driven in a straight line, F1 cars must also drive well around corners. Grand Prix cars can be driven around corners at far higher speeds than other racing cars.

Accidents such as this one, involving David Coulthard, are a reminder of the dangers of F1 racing.

The world watched as Lewis began his first **Formula One** season in 2007. Where would he end up after the 17 **Grand Prix** races throughout the year? Would he make it to the end? Even before he began the season, Lewis crashed a car while practising!

Lewis began the championship well. He came third in the first race, but in a practice session before the Monaco Grand Prix, he hit the barriers and damaged his car. Things got better when Lewis won two races in June, each one giving him ten points towards his total. The motor racing world was amazed when he took over the lead position in points, just a few above his teammate Fernando Alonso. Then, disappointment struck as Lewis had to retire from the Chinese Grand Prix. He had to abandon his car when it ended up in the gravel with tyre problems.

Final race in Brazil

At the start of the final race in Brazil, Lewis was ahead on points in the drivers' championship. He finished the final race seventh, however, and Ferrari driver Kimi Räikkönen beat Lewis by one point to take the championship. Afterwards Lewis said, "To think I have come from GP2 and I am now ranked two in the world is a positive thing. I go into next year full of confidence."

Lewis always wears his famous yellow crash helmet in Formula One races.

LEWIS HAMILTON'S FIRST YEAR OF FORMULA ONE GRAND PRIX RACES

Grand Prix	Date	Race position	Points	Total
Australia	18 Mar 2007	3	6	6
Malaysia	08 Apr 2007	2	8	14
Bahrain	15 Apr 2007	2	8	22
Spain	13 May 2007	2	8	30
Monaco	27 May 2007	2	8	38
Canada	10 Jun 2007	1	10	48
United States	17 Jun 2007	1	10	58
France	01 Jul 2007	3	6	64
Britain	08 Jul 2007	3	6	70
Europe	22 Jul 2007	9	0	70
Hungary	05 Aug 2007	1	10	80
Turkey	26 Aug 2007	5	4	84
Italy	09 Sep 2007	2	8	92
Belgium	16 Sep 2007	4	5	97
Japan	30 Sep 2007	1	10	107
China	07 Oct 2007	retired	0	107
Brazil	21 Oct 2007	7	2	109

After finishing as runner-up in the 2007 drivers' championship, Lewis began his second year in Formula One in 2008 with great determination. "This year is going to be different," he said. "I don't have any doubts that I am going to do a good job, but it means something different. It means I want to win it."

The whole racing world believes that one day Lewis will achieve his dream.

Being in the newspapers all the time adds to the pressure on any sporting hero. Although Lewis seems to cope under pressure, he must feel the strain when the **media** expect him to win every race. Commentaries such as this, given just before the start of the Chinese **Grand Prix** in 2007, are a good example of the huge expectations placed on Lewis Hamilton:

"Hamilton took a huge stride towards completing his world championship dream after the McLaren driver took **pole** for tomorrow's Chinese Grand Prix with another superb performance. The 22-year-old could become the first **rookie** in **Formula One** history to win the title..."

Even though that race went wrong for Lewis, he still remained calm.

WHAT IS POLE POSITION?

A driver has pole position when they begin a race at the front of the **starting grid** – the best place to start the race. The term comes from horse racing where the number one starter begins the race next to the inside pole. To gain pole position in Formula One, a driver has to have the fastest lap time in the **qualification** stage.

In the news

Lewis was in the middle of a big spy story in 2007, although he was not involved himself. The Ferrari team accused the McLaren-Mercedes team of cheating. A Ferrari worker was blamed for passing secret technical information to McLaren-Mercedes. The case went to court and McLaren-Mercedes had to pay a record-breaking fine of £50.8 million. Lewis' team was in the news, but for the wrong reasons.

Lewis has taken part in television programmes, too. He swapped his Formula One car to drive a family car for the BBC's *Top Gear* show, where he had to complete a circuit in the fastest time possible. His time of 44 seconds on a wet track was very impressive!

Lewis is seen here at the National Television Awards with Top Gear *presenter Jeremy Clarkson.*

Success in motor racing usually brings great wealth. At one time Lewis and his dad had to work hard to earn enough to help him on his way. At last, with his **Formula One** career underway, Lewis' fame led to fortune. Newspapers report that he is likely to become one of the highest paid sportsmen ever.

In his first year in Formula One, it is reported that Lewis earned £400,000, although bonus payments probably made this more than £1 million. Some newspapers report that Lewis could earn as much as £150 million in wages alone for a five-year deal, making him the highest-paid driver ever.

*Here Lewis launches a mobile Internet service for one of his **sponsors**.*

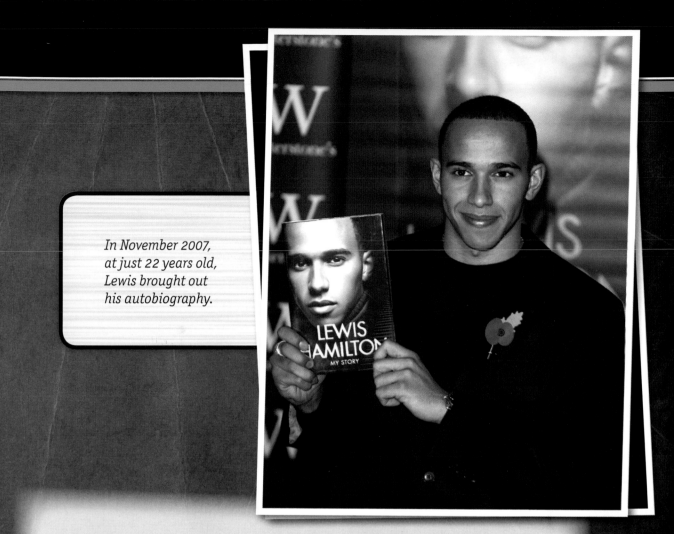

In November 2007, at just 22 years old, Lewis brought out his autobiography.

In his own words

Lewis made many headlines in 2007, but not all for his racing. He also signed a book deal to write his **autobiography**. In *My Story*, Lewis describes his amazing rise to the top of the motor racing world. He talks about the ups and downs of his first Formula One season, including the rivalry with Spanish teammate, Fernando Alonso.

Lewis' book tells what it was like to become the youngest driver ever to lead the championship before finally coming second. But his story isn't just about cars, competitions, winning, and glory. He tells of his special relationship with both his father and younger brother, Nicholas, who has **cerebral palsy**. Despite all the fame, fortune, and fuss about his success, it seems Lewis can still keep his feet firmly on the ground.

Fame and fortune can easily go to a person's head. People have often commented on how "grounded" and mature Lewis seems for his age. Lewis has answered: "I think the reason for that is that since I was 10, I was at the race track every weekend. I wasn't hanging out and doing stuff with my friends. I was with Dad and I had to be best friends with my dad." By mixing with so many adults in racing, he had to learn fast. "It's tough growing up and missing your childhood, because you never get it back, but if I make it I can have all the toys that I want!"

Lewis' brother Nicholas, who has **cerebral palsy**, often watches Lewis race. Lewis describes Nicholas as his inspiration. "He's always positive, he never complains about what he has. He just keeps his chin up." Whenever Lewis feels the pressure, he thinks about how many problems in life his brother has. "Nick can't do half the things that I can do and yet he's always happy. I think that's a strong message. Having him as a brother has a major effect on the way that I think."

Lewis' go-kart was auctioned for £42,100 on eBay for the baby charity "Tommy's".

Supporting others

Many sports stars know their success gives them a responsibility. Not only do many young people look up to them as **role models**, but their fame can also be used to help others. Many sports stars do a lot of work for charity. Lewis has also spent time raising money for good causes. He even sold his old go-kart in an **auction** to raise funds.

Great Ormond Street Children's Hospital is the official charity for the British **Grand Prix** and every year many of the patients at the hospital go to a party to meet their **Formula One** heroes. They all want to meet Lewis!

Lewis shows young karting hopefuls how to reach their racing dreams at the Daytona circuit in Milton Keynes.

Many young people dream of becoming a celebrity. But being famous has its bad points, particularly when newspapers are hunting for gossip. Lewis has had to learn that he will be followed and spied on, and his photograph will appear in newspapers. The stories can often be about his private life.

Friends or enemies?

Headlines have told of rows between Lewis and Fernando Alonso, even though the two drivers insist they are good friends. "They have been saying many things about us but they were not true," Alonso said at a press conference in Brazil before the final **Grand Prix** of 2007. Lewis also tried to put the record straight. Even though they might be rivals on the track, he said, "We had a very good relationship from day one. I think we've got on quite well this year despite what the **media** have said. They have always tried to put a big gap between us but they have not succeeded. We continue to do our job." Alonso returned to Renault in 2008, so the media had less to write about.

*The **media** tried to show that teammates Lewis Hamilton and Fernando Alonso were bitter rivals, but both drivers claimed they got on well.*

Lewis has to cope with photographers following him wherever he goes.

The positive side

Negative stories about Lewis' life must be difficult for him and his family to deal with, but there is also a positive side to fame and success. Lewis now earns a lot of money, which in some ways gives him more freedom than he had before. He can now afford great holidays and a better lifestyle. His sporting success can help to repay his dad for all the support he gave Lewis to get to where he is today. Lewis also gets to help people in need through his charity work. Some people say that Lewis' success story has breathed new life into a sport that needed revival.

It can be hard at the top. The challenge for anyone in sport is to keep ahead and to keep improving. Motor sport is particularly competitive and there will be many challenges ahead for Lewis. As he once said himself, "Every year [...] there are certain ways you have to up your game and interact with the team. Each year you analyse your last season. And then you try to improve that further."

Big questions face every racing driver such as:
• What will the following season bring?
• Will another team want to sign me up in the near future?
• In such a fast and dangerous sport, how safe will the next lap be?

Lewis once said: "I really don't know what it is that makes me so good. I just believe if there's one thing I'm meant to do really well, it's racing."

Lewis holds his 2007 World Championship trophy as the second place driver overall.

Lewis finishes first in the Australian Grand Prix in Melbourne, 2008.

Where next?

Lewis once said, after wining a race, "I was trying to control myself because I just wanted to park the car and jump out and do cartwheels. The next dream is to win the world championship."

Lewis Hamilton's success isn't due just to luck and having a great car. He has great skill, focus, determination, concentration, and self-control, as well as natural talent. He has managed to take on some of the best drivers in the world, usually much older than him. He's even beaten them on race tracks he has never seen before.

"I'm just having a fantastic day," Lewis said after one of his victories. "This is history." Most people agree that Lewis Hamilton will continue to make **Formula One** history.

1985 Lewis Carl Hamilton is born in Stevenage, Hertfordshire.

1995 Cadet Class: Lewis is Super One British Kart Champion.

1996 Cadet Class: Lewis wins the McLaren-Mercedes Champions of the Future series.

1998 Lewis is signed by McLaren-Mercedes to their Young Driver Support Programme.

2000 Formula A: Lewis is European Champion, World Cup Champion, and is awarded Karting World Number 1.

2001 Lewis begins car racing at the age of 16.
Lewis finishes fifth in the British Formula Renault winter series.
Lewis finishes third in Formula Renault UK Championship.

2002 British Formula Renault: Lewis finishes third with three wins, three fastest laps, and three **pole** positions.

2003 British Formula Renault: Lewis is champion with 10 wins; 9 fastest laps, and 11 pole positions.

2004 F3 **Euroseries**: Lewis wins the Bahrain F3 Superprix.

2005 F3 Euroseries: Lewis is champion with ASM F3 Dallara-Mercedes; winner of F3 Masters; winner of the Monaco F3 Grand Prix; winner of Pau F3 Grand Prix in France.

2006 GP2 Series: Lewis is champion with ART Grand Prix; winner of Monaco GP2 race; second double winner at Silverstone in a home race.

2007 Formula One: Lewis becomes driver for McLaren-Mercedes. He is runner up in the drivers' championship.

2008 Lewis moves to Switzerland. Lewis sets up the Lewis Hamilton Foundation charity.
Lewis signs a new five-year contract with McLaren-Mercedes.

FAST FACTS

 Lewis forgot he wasn't at work and drove too fast while in France at the end of 2007. His driving licence was suspended for a month after he was caught by the police. He was travelling at 196 kph (122 mph). The speed limit on French motorways is 130 kph (85 mph). He was also ordered to pay a £430 fine.

 Favourite music: hip-hop, R 'n' B, reggae, and funky house.

 Favourite musicians: The Roots, De La Soul, 2Pac, Biggie, Nas, Bob Marley, Sizzla, Sean Paul, Freddie McGregor, UB40, Chaka Demus & Pliers, Beenie Man, Sanchez, Warrior King.

 Lewis is a huge fan of reggae star Bob Marley and his sons Damian Marley and Ziggy Marley. He invited superstar rapper and producer Pharrell Williams as his guest to the 2007 US Grand Prix.

 Hobbies: music, playing the guitar, books, going to the gym, cycling, squash, tennis, karting, partying with friends, relaxing with family and friends, cinema, watching DVDs.

auction sale of items where people make bids. The person who makes the highest bid (offer of money) for the item gets to buy it.

autobiography person's life story, told by that person

black belt usually the highest belt colour awarded in martial arts, demonstrating a high level of skill

cerebral palsy condition resulting from damage to the brain, usually before or during birth, affecting the control of muscles and speech

cockpit space where a driver or pilot sits

Euroseries Europe-based junior racing car series of competitions in Formula Three racing

Formula One highest class of international motor racing

Grand Prix international motor races held as part of a world championship competition

media television, newspapers, magazines, and the Internet

podium stage where the top three finishing drivers stand after a race

pole position at the start of the race at the front of other cars

qualification (in Formula One) timed laps before a race, to decide positions on the starting grid

role model successful person whose behaviour is imitated by others, especially young people

rookie first-year player in a professional sport

sponsor company that pays money to a sportsperson in return for advertising their product

starting grid starting positions of cars on a race track

valet someone who cleans, washes, and polishes cars in a garage

Books

Designed for Success: Racing Cars (2nd Edition), Ian Graham (Heinemann Library, 2008)

The History of Formula One (Star Fire Guide), Ben Hunt (Flame Tree Publishing, 2007)

Lewis Hamilton: My Story, Lewis Hamilton (HarperCollins, 2007)

Lewis Hamilton: The Full Story, Mark Hughes (Icon Books Ltd, 2007)

Websites

www.Formula1.com
Find out all about Formula One racing at this site.

www.lewishamilton.com
Get up-to-date information on Lewis on his website.

www.mclaren.com
The McLaren-Mercedes website has all the latest news on the team that Lewis drives for.

www.buckmore.co.uk
Visit this site to find out more about Buckmore Park go-karting track, the karting track where Lewis Hamilton was discovered.

INDEX